I0816570

THIS BOOK IS PRESENTED TO:
ON:
BY:

Printed in China

First edition: 2023 10 9 8 7 6 5 4 3 2 1

Names: Parker, Amy, 1976-, author. | Nawrocki, Mike, author. | Thompson, Taylor, illustrator.

Title: Bible for me : stories and prayers / written by Amy Parker and Mike Nawrocki; illustrated by Taylor Thompson.

Description: Summary: Features 50 devotionals to help families grow in their faith together and come face-to-face with God's endless love for them, providing a firm foundation of faith to last a lifetime. A companion to The Bible for Me: Bible Stories and Prayers.

Identifiers: ISBN: 978-1-5710-2700-9

Subjects: LCSH Bible stories. | BISAC JUVENILE NONFICTION / Religion / Devotional Prayer

Classification: LCC BS551.2 .P372 2021 | DDC 220.9/505--dc23

Project management by Dan Lynch, Brentwood Press

Interior design by Diana Lawrence

Edited by Julie Monroe

Theological review by Doug Powell

Visit or contact us at TheBibleforMe.com

Mike Nawrocki
and Amy Parker
BIBLE STORIES & PRAYERS
FAMILY DEVOTIONAL
LEADING YOUR FAMILY THROUGH THE BIBLE FROM GENESIS TO REVELATION
Illustrated by
Taylor Thompson
BRENTWOOD
PRESS

Dear Reader,

Thank you for choosing to share these Bible stories. We know that an early understanding of God's Word plays a vital role in establishing a lifelong foundation of faith, and we thank you for making that a priority for the children in your life.

Bible Stories & Prayers, as part of the Bible for Me series, was written to speak directly to the listeners, your children, and to tell God's story in a way that reveals His love for each of them.

We hope not only to convey the original power and timelessness of each story, but also to emphasize how personal and relevant the story is to each child's life. Every story ends with a prayer that enables you (the reader) to substitute your child's name for the words marked in blue, making the story uniquely personal.

We hope that after reading *Bible Stories & Prayers* children will understand God's endless love for them, providing a firm foundation of faith to last a lifetime.

Here's an example of how you can make the prayers at the end of each story personal for your child.

Dear God,

Thank You for sending Jesus to take away our sins. Please help us always remember Him and what He has done for us. Amen.

Dear God,

Thank You for sending Jesus to take away our sins. Please help Amy always remember Him and what He has done for her. Amen.

Dear Child,

Do you know that God loves you and has a plan for you? He does! Do you know that He had His story written down for you? He did!

He loves you so much that over the entire history of God's people, He inspired His followers to write their story, His story. When we read this big story, we learn so much about who God is, about how our character should look like His, and how deep and wide and endless His love is for us.

In this book you and your family can learn from fifty stories from the Bible with short and fun devotionals that will help you understand the amazing characteristics of God and His Story. These devotionals go along with the stories in *The Bible for Me: Bible Stories and Prayers Bible Storybook* and will show you God's glorious power, His faithfulness, and how He has loved and guided His people. You'll find fun sections like "Did You Know," "Words to Know," "Talk About It," and "Do It" in each devotional to encourage you to learn and grow together as a family. As you read through the devotionals with your family you will all learn more about God, and you will see how the Bible is your story too.

As you read or listen to these devotionals and Bible stories, please remember that these words are for you, given to you by a God who loves you so very much.In His love,

Mike & Amy

Old Testament Bible Story Devotions

New Testament Bible Story Devotions

Close your eyes. What do you see?

That's pretty much what the universe looked like before God started creating. Genesis 1:2 tells us, "The earth was formless and empty" and "darkness was over the surface of the deep" (NIV). But the next part changed everything.

When God spoke over that empty void, the earth was filled with shimmering light and tall trees with juicy oranges and meadows of gorgeous lilies and sprinting gazelles and dazzling peacocks and tiny little ants. He made it all, from the very beginning.

After He created the perfect landscape, filling it with life, He said, "Let's make humans in Our image." And into the dust, God breathed new life, and the first human exhaled the breath of God.

Can you believe it? God thought of us and created us and breathed His very own breath into us. And the whole time He had the perfect plan, that through Jesus, we could be with Him for all eternity.

God has always been here—even before the very beginning. And if we believe in His Son, Jesus, we will be with Him always, even after the very end.God has always been here—even before the very beginning. And if we believe in His Son, Jesus, we will be with Him always, even after the very end.

Dear God,

Wow! You created such an amazing world–and even more amazing humans! Thank You for thinking of us and making us. Help us to take care of this world and our bodies that were created from Your very own breath. Most importantly, Thank You for making a way for us to live with You forever! Amen.

DO IT!

Go outside today and stand in God's amazing creation. Look at how incredible and wonderful it is, and know that He made *you* that way too!

Adam and Eve Mess Up

(Genesis 2–3)

DID YOU KNOW?
God has loved us from the very beginning, even when we choose to do wrong!

Have you ever chosen to do something that you knew wasn't right? Maybe you broke your brother's toy and hid it in the trash. Maybe you snuck a cookie after Mom told you not to eat any. Or maybe you were mean to the girl next door.

Doing what we know is wrong, what goes against what God tells us to do, is called *sin*. And sin has been around ever since Adam and Eve were in the garden of Eden. The truth is, we all mess up just like they did (Romans 3:23), but that doesn't mean it's okay. Sin is just as wrong today as it was way back in the very beginning.

So, how do we fix it? Well, we can't. But God can.

WORDS TO KNOW!

Then the LORD God called to the man, "Where are you?" Genesis 3:9 NLT

When Adam and Eve messed up, they ran and hid—as if God couldn't find them! But God called for them, and they stepped out from behind the trees and told Him what they had done. Yes, they still got in trouble! But *absolutely* yes, God still loved them and cared for them.

TALK ABOUT IT!

How do you act when you've done something wrong? What does God want us to do?

God loves us so much that He made a plan for when we mess up. He sent His very own Son, Jesus, to earth to bear the cost of all our sins. God looks for us (Luke 15), even though we are sinners, just like He looked for Adam and Eve. And if we believe in Jesus, we can go to God and ask for the forgiveness that only Jesus can give.

Dear God,

Thank You for sending Jesus to pay the price for our sins. Please help us to choose right over wrong, and please forgive us for our sins. Thank You for loving us and caring for us even when we do wrong. Amen.

DO IT!

Read Luke 15:3–7 with your family. Then play a game of hide-and-seek, remembering how Jesus, our Good Shepherd, looks for His sheep.

3

God Starts Over

(Genesis 6-9)

What would you do if God asked you to do something for Him that sounded really hard?

DID YOU KNOW?
You can always trust God!

That's what happened with Noah. In Genesis 6:14–15, God told Noah, "Build a large boat from cypress wood and waterproof it with tar, inside and out. Then construct decks and stalls throughout the interior. Make the boat 450 feet long, 75 feet wide, and 45 feet high" (NLT). That's huge! A boat that big is way longer than a football field and taller than a four-story building.

God gave Noah these instructions so that he and his family and two of every kind of animal would be saved from a big flood. The Bible tells us that God had mercy on Noah because Noah loved and trusted God.

WORDS TO KNOW!

So Noah did everything exactly as God had commanded him.
Genesis 6:22 NLT

Do you think God would ask you to build a big boat? Probably not. But because He loves you, He does give you instructions. He asks you to believe in His Son, Jesus, He asks you to pray and read His Word, and He asks you to always love others.

Sometimes doing those things can feel as difficult as building a huge boat. But, like Noah, when we trust and obey God, He will take care of us too!

TALK ABOUT IT!

If you took a ride on Noah's ark, what animals would you like to care for?

Dear God,

Thank You for saving Noah and his family and all the animals. We know we can always trust You. Please help us to be able to do the things You ask us to do. And thank You for saving us when we believe in Your Son, Jesus. Amen.

DO IT!

Animals are amazing, aren't they? If you have a pet, do something to help take care of it: feed your cat, take your dog on a walk, clean your rhinoceros's horn. If you don't have a pet, just go outside and listen to the birds sing and thank God for making animals.

4 God's Promise to Abraham

(Genesis 12-13, 15, 17-18, 21)

If your dad promised to turn you into an elephant, you would laugh, right? And if your friend promised to clean your room by snapping her fingers, you would wonder how she could make that happen, wouldn't you?

When Abraham and Sarah were much too old to have children, God promised them they would do just that. And to Sarah and Abraham, that seemed just as impossible as Dad turning you into an elephant. Sarah laughed and Abraham wondered. But God said, "Is anything too hard for Me to do?"

DID YOU KNOW?
God always keeps His promises–even when they seem impossible!

WORDS TO KNOW!
Is anything too difficult for the LORD? Genesis 18:14 NASB

The answer, of course, is no. About a year later, Sarah and Abraham had that baby boy, fulfilling another promise God had made to Abraham, that he would be the father of a great nation, the Israelites (Genesis 12:1–3).

Did you know that God has made you promises too? The Bible is full of them, thousands of them! He promises to watch over us (Psalm 32:8), to love us (Isaiah 54:10 NIV), and He even promises to keep His promises (Deuteronomy 7:9).

So when you're feeling unsteady or uncertain about what lies ahead, dig in to your Bible and look for some of those promises that God has made to you. No matter what else is going on, the one thing you can trust, without a doubt, is that God will keep His promises—even when they seem impossible.

Dear God,

Thank You for making us promises that we can rely on—even the ones that sound impossible. Please help us to trust in You before we put our trust in anyone or anything else. Thank You for doing the impossible. Amen.

DO IT!

Find one of your favorite promises in the Bible and write it down. Color it, decorate it, and hang it up for everyone to see. Let it be a reminder of the promises that God keeps.

5

Abraham Gives His Best

(Genesis 22)

DID YOU KNOW?
God wants our very best!

What does it mean to give your best? Does it mean to try your hardest? Does it mean giving the most? Does it mean giving the first and most important of what you have?

Really it can mean all of these things. For Abraham, it was being willing to give up the thing he loved the most, his very own son (Genesis 22:2). For Abel, it was bringing "the best parts of his best sheep" (Genesis 4:4 ICB). For the widow at the temple, it was giving two tiny copper coins, but it was all she had (Luke 21). For us, it could be something completely different.

WORDS TO KNOW!

The LORD says, "Because you did not keep back your son, your only son, from me, I make you this promise by my own name: I will surely bless you and give you many descendants."
Genesis 22:16–17 NCV

God is holy, and everything we have is all His anyway. So when we worship Him, when we give offerings to Him, when we serve others in His name, we should always bring the best to Him. It could be giving our time, our money, or our gifts. But whatever it is, it should be our very best. And if giving our best ever starts to feel like too much, we can remember the sacrifice He gave for us: His very own Son, to save us from our sins.

Your best may look different from your parents' best. Your best may look like less than your friend's. But as He did with the widow and her two copper coins, God knows our hearts. And He knows when we're offering up our very best.

TALK ABOUT IT!

What does it look like for you to give your best to God?

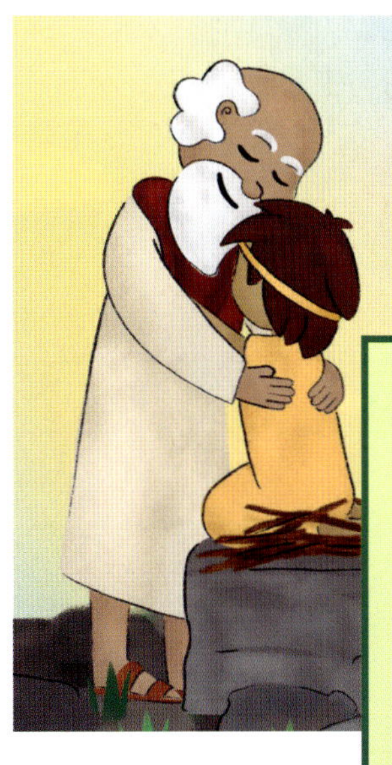

Dear God,

Help us to put You first in everything we do. When we work for You, when we worship You, help us always to offer our best. Thank You for giving Your best to us. Amen.

DO IT!

Think of a way that you can offer up your best to God today. Whether it's focused prayer time, helping a neighbor, or giving part of your allowance, give your best back to God today.

6 Jacob's and Esau's Blessings

(Genesis 24–25, 27)

Back when Jacob and Esau were born, the firstborn son received the greatest blessing from his father. That son would inherit what his parents had, and the father would speak a special blessing from God over his life.

DID YOU KNOW?
God Knows our future!

But before Jacob and Esau were born, God told their mother, Rebekah, that she was having twins and that the older son would serve the younger son. In the end, Rebekah and Isaac would see both of those things come true for their twin boys. Jacob, the younger brother, would have twelve sons, who would become the twelve tribes of Israel, God's chosen people.

Just as God knew the future of Jacob and Esau before they were even born, He knows our future too. He has created us for a purpose and prepared things for us to do (Ephesians 2:10). So how do we know what those things are?

WORDS TO KNOW!

The LORD told her, "The sons in your womb will become two nations. . . . One nation will be stronger than the other; and your older son will serve your younger son." Genesis 25:23 NLT

Well, we can do like Rebekah did and talk to God. When Rebekah had questions, she simply asked God about them (Genesis 25:22). And God has invited us to do the same. The Bible says, "If any of you lacks wisdom, you should ask God, who gives generously to all without finding fault, and it will be given to you" (James 1:5 NIV). That doesn't mean we'll hear His answer in the same way we'd hear a parent or a friend, but you can be certain that God hears your every prayer and will answer in ways that only He can.

TALK ABOUT IT!

What do you think God has planned for your future?

Dear God,

Thank You for knowing and planning our future. Thank You for hearing our every prayer. Please help **us** to remember Your promise to give wisdom when **we** need it. Amen.

DO IT!

As a family, talk to God about His plans for each of you. Then write down any big dreams or goals you may have and what steps it may take to get there. As your dreams and goals continue to take shape, be sure to check in with God and change them as He directs your paths.

7 Joseph Helps His Brothers

(Genesis 37, 39-45)

Do you have older brothers or sisters? Older cousins or friends? Do they ever treat you in a way that's not so good?

Well, when Joseph was young, his brothers sold him to some traders and told their father that he had been killed. The men who bought Joseph took him far from home and sold him to a man in Egypt. Sounds pretty bad, huh?

The sad truth is that people are not always going to treat us well. There will be people who are dishonest, rude, and downright mean. But we can trust God to make those bad things work out for our good, just as He did for Joseph. Romans 8:28 tells us, "And we know that in all things God works for the good of those who love him, who have been called according to his purpose" (NIV).

WORDS TO KNOW!

"You meant to hurt me, but God turned your evil into good to save the lives of many people."
Genesis 50:20 NCV

In the end, because Joseph was in Egypt—and God was with Joseph—he was able to save his family during a famine, when there was very little food in the land. Joseph forgave his brothers and brought them to live with him in Egypt where they would have plenty of everything. Through it all, Joseph followed God, and God worked out Joseph's horrible situation for the good of everyone.

TALK ABOUT IT!

Have you ever seen something bad work out for your good?

Dear God,

We're so glad that You're in control and working out everything for our good. Help us always to remember, even when things look bad, that You're working out everything for the good of those who love You. Amen.

DO IT!

Make a list of some bad situations happening right now. Then talk to God about every one of them, asking Him to help work out those situations for the good of those who love Him.

8 Baby Moses Is Saved

(Exodus 1–2)

DID YOU KNOW?
God is always watching over us!

Moses's mom faced a very scary situation. She couldn't keep baby Moses hidden any longer. But she knew that if the pharaoh or his men saw the baby, Moses would not survive because of the new law that the pharaoh had made.

She sadly, faithfully placed her precious baby in a floating basket and hid him in the river grass. Moses's sister, Miriam, watched in amazement as the princess found Moses and took him to be her own, to be raised in the pharaoh's own palace!

God is always, *always* watching over His people. He loves us so much and can save us in so many miraculous ways. And even more than that, He will go on to use us as part of His big plans—just as He did with Moses!

WORDS TO KNOW!

God saw the troubles of the people of Israel, and he was concerned about them.
Exodus 2:25 ICB

So whenever you're scared or worried or anxious, just think of baby Moses in a basket and how God kept him safe. And remember that God—who made the universe and everyone in it—is also watching over *you*.

Dear God,

Thank You for always watching over us. Thank You for keeping us safe, even and especially when we feel afraid. Amen.

DO IT!

Whenever you feel worried, anxious, or afraid, what are you going to do about it? Make a plan today!

9

God Calls Moses

(Exodus 2-4)

When God called to Moses through a burning bush, He told Moses how He would use him to save His people. But Moses had a whole lot of excuses for God about why he couldn't do what God asked of him. "I'm a nobody! And I'm not a good speaker! Nobody will believe me!"

DID YOU KNOW?

God always helps us to do His work!

That's when God reminded Moses of who He was. "Who created you? Who created the mouth so you could speak?" God said. "I will be with you. Tell the people that God has sent you!"

WORDS TO KNOW!

"Who gave human beings their mouths? . . . Is it not I, the LORD? Now go; I will help you speak and will teach you what to say." Exodus 4:11–12 NIV

TALK ABOUT IT!
What do you love to do?
How could God use that
for His purposes?

Did you know that God has a calling, a purpose for us all? Paul wrote, "He has saved us and called us with a holy calling, not according to our works, but according to His own purpose and grace" (2 Timothy 1:9 HCSB).

So before we get any big ideas about what we can and cannot do with our lives, maybe we should talk to God about it first. He has given us everything we need (Hebrews 13:21) to do exactly what He has called us to do!

Dear God,

Thank You for giving us everything we need to fulfill Your purposes. Help us always to seek You and Your purposes and to do what You have created us to do. Amen.

DID YOU KNOW?

Go do something that you love to do. While you're doing it, think of all of the ways that God has equipped you to do that very thing.

10 God Splits the Red Sea

(Exodus 4–15)

We can get so overwhelmed by the world around us that we forget how powerful our God is! That's what happened to Moses and the Israelites. They were standing at the edge of the Red Sea with a whole bunch of heavily armed soldiers rushing toward them. They were trapped! They panicked!

DID YOU KNOW?
The Lord will fight for you!

But Moses—he talked to God. And in that quick conversation, God gave Moses the solution: "Raise your staff above the sea." When Moses did that simple thing, the power of God went into action, blowing back the waters of the sea, creating a dry path for the Israelites to cross. And eventually, those same waters washed away the army trying to defeat God's people.

WORDS TO KNOW!

"The LORD himself will fight for you. Just stay calm." Exodus 14:14 NLT

God hasn't stopped fighting for His people. In little ways and in big ways, every day He is fighting for us too. He can cure illnesses. He can stop evil plans. He can prompt us to look one more time before crossing the road. When you are facing a battle bigger than yourself, stop and talk to the One who has already overcome the world (John 16:33). He will fight for you!

TALK ABOUT IT!

Either in the Bible or in your own life, how have you seen God fight for His people?

Dear God,

Thank You for fighting for us. When we are overwhelmed or afraid, help us to remember all of the ways that You are going to battle for us every day. Amen.

DO IT!

Create a battle plan. Write down some scary or difficult things you are facing right now. Then find Bible verses that help you to remember how God will fight for you. Be sure to write those down too and read them whenever you're getting ready for battle!

11

Moses on the Mountain

(Exodus 19–20)

DID YOU KNOW?
God gives us rules because He love us!

Has your mom or dad ever asked you to do something, or not to do something? Why do you think your parents tell you what to do? If your mom says, "Wash your hands before you eat that pizza!" or your dad tells you, "Don't play with that wild monkey!" it's not because your mom doesn't want you to enjoy that delicious pizza or because your dad doesn't appreciate your love of primates. It's because your mom doesn't want you to get sick and your dad wants you to keep all your hair. They love you and want what's best for you.

God brought the Israelites out of Egypt and delivered them from slavery. God told them, "I carried you on eagles' wings and brought you to myself" (Exodus 19:4 NLT). God loved His people and wanted what was best for them so He also gave them a list of rules to live by. By following God's commandments, the people of Israel would learn more about how perfect and holy God is, and how much they needed Him to save them.

And through Israel, Jesus would one day save the whole world!

Isn't it cool that the first four commandments are about loving God and the second six commandments are about loving people? God knows what's best for us: to love Him and to love others!

And just like you are better off when you follow your parents' rules, we are all better off when we follow His commandments!

TALK ABOUT IT!

Is it possible to keep all of the commandments all of the time?

Dear God,

Thank You for giving us Your commandments. Thank You for loving us and wanting what is best for us. Help us to love You and love each other. And most of all, thank You for saving us by sending us Your Son, Jesus. Amen.

DO IT!

Can you name all the Ten Commandments from memory? Write each commandment on an index card, then see if you can memorize them.

Loving God Commandments:

- You must have no other god before God.
- Do not make idols to worship.
- Do not misuse God's name.
- Dedicate one day a week to resting and worshiping God.

Loving Others Commandments:

- Honor your father and mother.
- Do not murder.
- Be faithful to your wife or husband.
- Do not steal from each other.
- Do not lie to each other.
- Do not be jealous of each other.

12

Exploring Canaan

(Numbers 13-14)

What do you see when you face a new situation? Do you see all the dangers and all the things that could go wrong? Or can you find the beauty and blessings? Maybe a little bit of both?

When Moses sent out a group to explore the land that God was giving them, most of the men came back moaning and complaining when they saw the people who already lived there. "Those guys will squish us like grasshoppers! We can never take this land!"

DID YOU KNOW?

God wants the very best for His people!

But Joshua and Caleb told the Israelites about the richness of the land. They had brought back grapes and pomegranates and figs. Believing in God's promises, they said, "If God wants to give us this land, He can and He will!" God rewarded Joshua and Caleb for their faithfulness.

WORDS TO KNOW!

"If the LORD is pleased with us, he will lead us into that land, a land flowing with milk and honey, and will give it to us." Numbers 14:8 NIV

God wants to give the very best to His people. But we're not likely to see the best He has to offer if we're not looking for it, if we're not believing in His promises, if we're always expecting the worst. When God makes you promises, you can always believe them—and you can always be looking for His best!

TALK ABOUT IT!

What are some ways that God has provided for your family?

Dear God,

Thank You for rewarding us with Your best when we are obedient to You. Help **us** always to believe in Your promises and to look for Your best in **our** lives. Amen.

DO IT!

On your next trip to the grocery story, buy some grapes, pomegranates, or figs. Eat them and think about how God has provided for *you* in the land He has given you, just as He did for the Israelites.

13

Joshua and the Big Wall

(Joshua 6)

Has your brother or sister ever been mean to you? Have you ever been pushed by a kid at school? Does it make you want to be mean or push right back? After all, you didn't do anything wrong; who would blame you for defending yourself? If someone were to tell you, "Love people who are

DID YOU KNOW?
We can always follow God's instructions—even when they sound strange!

WORDS TO KNOW!
"For my thoughts are not your thoughts, neither are your ways my ways," declares the LORD. "As the heavens are higher than the earth, so are my ways higher than your ways and my thoughts than your thoughts." Isaiah 55:8–9 NIV

mean to you and pray for those who mistreat you," would you think that sounded a little strange?

Marching around a city thirteen times, blowing horns, and shouting may have sounded like a strange plan to Joshua for bringing down a big wall, but he knew that God's ways were not man's ways. Joshua knew that following God's instructions is always the best thing to do, so that was what he did. And the walls fell down!

Would being kind to your brother make sense right after he ate the last brownie that was supposed to be yours? In the Sermon on the Mount, Jesus told His followers, "Love your enemies and pray for those who persecute you." (Not that your brownie-eating brother is your actual enemy, but he might feel like one as he munched away.) You can let your brother know you are disappointed, but treating him kindly in spite of his actions is the right thing to do.

DO IT!

Do something kind for your brother or sister or someone in your family today.

TALK ABOUT IT!

Can you think of other stories in the Bible where God gave instructions that must have seemed strange? (Here's one hint: Who built a giant boat in the middle of dry land?

Dear God,

We thank You that Your way is always the best way. Please help **us** follow Your directions even when **we** might want to do things differently. Amen.

Gideon and the Tiny Army

(Judges 6-7)

Have you ever needed to do something that you didn't think you could do, like swimming all the way across the pool for the first time or trying to fall asleep on Christmas Eve? Did you pray and ask God for help?

God wants us to look to Him for help!

WORDS TO KNOW!

I lift up my eyes to the mountains—where does my help come from? My help comes from the LORD, the Maker of heaven and earth. Psalm 121:1-2 NIV

God wanted Gideon to do something very difficult: to defeat a whole army! An angel appeared to Gideon and said, "Mighty hero, the Lord is with you!" (Judges 6:12 NLT). Gideon could hardly believe it. He thought, *I'm the weakest kid in my family!*

But you know what? It didn't matter, because in the end it wasn't Gideon who defeated the army. It was God! All Gideon needed to do was to trust God and look to Him for help.

God wants us to look to Him for help with everything—the hard things and even the easy things. If we look to Him in everything we do, He'll be with us. You are a mighty hero when the Lord is with you!

TALK ABOUT IT!

Do you think you can trust God the way Gideon did?

DO IT!

Draw a picture of yourself as a mighty hero!

Dear God,

Please help us to look to You for help, with the big things and the small things. Thank You for always helping us. Amen.

15

God Calls Samuel

(1 Samuel 1–3)

We saw God call Moses way back in Exodus, and then He called Joshua and Gideon too. God can only use grown-ups to do His work, right? Wrong!

When Samuel was just a young boy studying in the temple, God called to him. Even though Samuel was studying God's law and practicing His rules, he still was surprised that God was calling him. He was so surprised that he didn't even think it was God. He thought it was Eli, the priest, calling from the other room.

DID YOU KNOW?
God calls us to do His work!

But as soon as Samuel realized—with a little help from Eli—that the voice calling him was the voice of God Himself, Samuel got quiet and listened. He not only listened, but he answered God as an obedient servant.

WORDS TO KNOW!

The LORD came and called as before, "Samuel! Samuel!" And Samuel replied, "Speak, your servant is listening." 1 Samuel 3:10 NLT

God can use us all—right here, right now, no matter what age we are! He doesn't always speak with a voice we can hear with our ears. He speaks through His Word. He speaks to us through wise teachers and leaders. And He speaks to us through prayer and the Holy Spirit. Our job, first and foremost, is to listen and obey.

TALK ABOUT IT!

What are some ways that God speaks to us? How has He spoken to you?

Dear God,

Thank You for calling us all–no matter our age–to be a part of Your plan. Help us to listen for Your voice and to answer when You call. Amen.

DO IT!

Start keeping a journal and list the things that God has said to you through prayer, through His Word, or through the wisdom of those around you. Review your list often and be sure to obey!

16

David Fights a Giant

(1 Samuel 17)

No one knows exactly how big Goliath was, but most likely he was around eight feet tall and weighed four hundred and fifty pounds. That's a really big dude! If you invited Goliath over for dinner, he would have to duck down and turn sideways to fit through your front door. Can you imagine facing off against someone as big as Goliath?

DID YOU KNOW?

Even though you might be little, God is big and mighty!

But you know what? David was not afraid of Goliath in the least! There were two reasons for this. The first one is that David was an expert with his sling. As a shepherd, he went up against big lions and bears to protect his sheep. The second, and the most important reason, was that David trusted that God would take care of him. He told King Saul, "The LORD who rescued me from the paw of the lion and the paw of the bear will rescue me from the hand of this Philistine!" (1 Samuel 17:37 NIV).

WORDS TO KNOW!

The Lord rescues the godly; he is their fortress in times of trouble.
Psalm 37:39 NLT

When you're facing something big, even as big as a giant, you don't have to be afraid because God is even bigger. He is your fortress in times of trouble!

TALK ABOUT IT!

Is there anything you are afraid of? Do you think God is bigger than that?

DO IT!

Get your parents' help to measure and mark a line on a tree at eight feet tall. Can you jump up and touch it? That's pretty tall, right?

Dear God,

Thank You loving us. Thank You that **we** can always look to You in times of trouble and that You are always bigger than **our** biggest problems. Amen.

17 Jonathan Helps His Best Friend

(1 Samuel 18, 20)

Aren't friends amazing? It's so much fun getting to hang out, talk to, and play with someone who understands you and likes a lot of the same things you like, isn't it? And if you have a best friend, that's even better. Best friends are with you in both good times and tough times, when you want to laugh and when you need to cry.

DID YOU KNOW?
God gives us friends to help each other!

After David defeated Goliath, David served King Saul and became best friends with Saul's son, Jonathan. Jonathan was a great friend to David—both in good times and in bad. At first, everything was great. David was very successful. But because of David's growing popularity among the people of Israel, King Saul grew jealous and wanted to kill him.

At first, Jonathan couldn't believe that his own dad would want to kill his best friend. But when Jonathan finally learned the truth, he helped David escape and saved his life. They promised always to be loyal to each other. Talk about good friends!

WORDS TO KNOW!

A friend is always loyal, and a brother is born to help in a time of need. Proverbs 17:17 NLT

For playing and for helping, true friends are a gift from God. What a great thing it is to have one and to be one.

TALK ABOUT IT!

Do you have a best friend? Who is it? What makes them your best friend?

DO IT!

Tell a friend how awesome they are and how thankful you are to be their friend!

Dear God,

Thank You for giving us friends. Please help us to be a good friend, in good times and in tough times, like Jonathan was to David. Amen.

18 A King After God's Own Heart

(1 Samuel 16; 2 Samuel 2)

What do you think your life will look like when you grow up? What kind of person will you be? Will you have a family with kids of your own? Will you be a teacher or a firefighter or a singer? It's fun to dream about what the future holds, but God already knows. He knows everything about you—everything you are doing now and everything you will do. He even knew you before you were born!

DID YOU KNOW?
God has a plan for your life!

When David was very young, before he fought Goliath or served King Saul, God told the prophet Samuel that He wanted a new king for Israel. Even though David was the youngest and the smallest of his brothers, God saw David's heart and knew he would be the best person for the job. Samuel anointed David with oil and proclaimed that he would one day be the king.

Fifteen years later, when David turned thirty, Samuel's proclamation came true and David became king.

WORDS TO KNOW!

You saw me before I was born. Every day of my life was recorded in your book. Every moment was laid out before a single day had passed. Psalm 139:16 NLT

One day you'll be bigger too. You probably won't be a king or a queen, but maybe you'll be a president or the head of a company. Whatever your future holds, isn't it great to know that God already knows and has a plan for you?

TALK ABOUT IT!

Talk to your mom and dad about when they were kids. What did they think their future would look like? Can they see how God worked in their lives?

DO IT!

Dream of what your future will look like. Write it down and seal it in an envelope to read when you grow up.

Dear God,

Thank You that our life and future are in Your hands. Please help us trust You and follow Your plan for us. Amen.

19

The Wise King

(1 Kings 3)

If you had one wish to get anything you wanted, what would it be? To have a closet packed with all the best toys? To get a new puppy? When King David's son Solomon became king, God asked Solomon a question: "What do you want? Ask and I will give it to you." What do you think Solomon asked for?

DID YOU KNOW?

God will give you wisdom. All you have to do is ask!

As a king, Solomon might have asked for lots of money, a long life, or help defeating his enemies. But instead, Solomon asked God for "an understanding heart so that I can govern your people well and know the difference between right and wrong" (1 Kings 3:9 NLT). Solomon asked for wisdom to be the best king. This made God very happy.

If fact, God answered Solomon, "I will give you what you asked for! . . . And I will also give you what you have not asked for—riches and fame . . . and a long life" (1 Kings 3:12–14 NLT). Solomon put God and others first, and God loved that!

WORDS TO KNOW!

How much better to get wisdom than gold, and good judgement than silver! Proverbs 16:16 NLT

God will also give you wisdom. All you have to do is ask Him. The Bible says, "If you need wisdom, ask our generous God, and he will give it to you" (James 1:5 NLT). Wisdom will help you make good choices, know the difference between right and wrong, and better serve God and others.

TALK ABOUT IT!

Ask your friends what they would wish for if they could have anything. Could it be better than wisdom?

Dear God,

Thank You for giving us everything we need. Thank You for being so loving and so generous. Please also give us wisdom. Amen.

DO IT!

Make a wise choice today. Should you eat two ice cream cones or just one? Should you do your homework right away or wait until later?

The One True God

(1 Kings 18)

Have you ever been camping in the mountains and looked up into the night sky? Maybe you've done that in your own backyard. If there aren't a lot of clouds or nearby house and street lights, you can easily see thousands of stars. If you have a small telescope,

DID YOU KNOW?

God is more powerful than anyone or anything!]

you can see millions. If you could look through a space telescope, you'd see so many stars, they'd be impossible to count.

Our star, the sun, is one of one hundred billion stars in the Milky Way galaxy. And the Milky Way is one of two trillion galaxies, each containing billions of stars. Are you dizzy with numbers yet?

But as big as the universe is, it's not bigger than God. He created all things in heaven and on earth. Can you imagine challenging God to a contest? That would be a silly thing to do, right? When King Ahab's god, Baal, didn't show up for a contest, Elijah joked, "Maybe he's taking a nap or going to the bathroom?" When Elijah called on the name of the Lord, He appeared right away and showed everyone that He is the one true God.

WORDS TO KNOW!

Yours, O LORD, is the greatness, the power, the glory, the victory, and the majesty. Everything in the heavens and on earth is yours, O LORD, and this is your Kingdom. We adore you as the one who is over all things.
1 Chronicles 29:11 NLT

Imagine—the one true God, who created the universe and all of the countless stars, also made you and loves you!

Dear God,

Everything in heaven and on earth is Yours. You are the one true God. Thank You for creating **us** and for loving **us**. Amen.

DO IT!

Go outside tonight and look up to the sky. How many stars can you count?

21 Elisha, the Prophet's Apprentice

(1 Kings 19; 2 Kings 2, 4)

When you are hungry and ask your parents for a sandwich, do they give you a rock to eat instead? Of course not! They love you and know that a sandwich will be good for you. It will nourish your body and take away your hunger.

Your heavenly Father also wants to give you what is good for you. He wants to give you His gifts. And the wonderful thing about God's gifts is that they are good for both you and others.

DID YOU KNOW?

God will give us all we need to serve Him and help others!

Elisha was an assistant to Elijah, one of Israel's most important and gifted prophets. When the time had come for Elijah to go up to heaven in a chariot of fire, he asked Elisha what he wanted most of all. Elisha replied, "Please let me inherit a double share of your spirit and become your successor" (2 Kings 2:9 NLT). Elisha asked for double what God had given Elijah. He wanted to help people twice as much as Elijah had!

God granted his request. During his life, Elijah performed eight miracles. Elisha went on to perform sixteen, more than any other person in the Bible except Jesus. Elisha's wish was to serve God and others. He asked and he received!

WORDS TO KNOW!

"For anyone who asks, receives. Everyone who seeks, finds. And to everyone who knocks, the door will be opened." Matthew 7:8 NLT

How do you feel when you help others? It probably makes you feel great. Pray and ask God for opportunities to serve others. Ask and you will receive!

TALK ABOUT IT!

What is your favorite way to help others? How do you feel when you help them?

Dear God,

Please give us all that we need to serve You and help others. Amen.

DO IT!

Find a way to help someone in your family today.

The Girl Who Saved Her People

(Esther 1-10)

Have you ever felt like you are ordinary and there is nothing unique about you? Do you think, *If there are almost eight billion people in the world, how can I be special?*

But you know what? It doesn't matter how big the world is or how many people there are, there is only one you, and you fit perfectly into God's big plan!

DID YOU KNOW?
God has put you at the right place at the right time!

Esther was an ordinary girl, raised by her cousin Mordecai after her parents died. She was picked to be the queen by King Xerxes because of her beauty, but Ether's looks were not what made her special. Esther was special because she trusted in God's plan and wanted to be a part of it. For Esther, that meant risking her life by speaking out against the evil plans of Haman.

Esther could have chosen not to act, but instead, she realized that God had put her where He did for a reason. She chose to act bravely, and she became a hero who saved her people.

WORDS TO KNOW!

"If you keep quiet at a time like this, deliverance and relief for the Jews will arise from some other place, but you and your relatives will die. Who knows if perhaps you were made queen for just such a time as this?" Esther 4:14 NLT

Just like Esther, God can use you in His big plans. You just need to be willing to be a part of them. And that's what will make you special!

TALK ABOUT IT!

How is reading the Bible and praying important for knowing Gd's will for our lives?

Dear God,

Let Your will be done on earth as it is in heaven. Thank You for making us part of Your plan and please help us to always follow You. Amen.

DO IT!

The Jewish holiday of Purim is celebrated every year sometime in February or March. Hamantaschen cookies, a traditional food served during Purim, are named after the villain of the story of Esther, Haman. With your parents' help, find a recipe, bake some cookies, and eat 'em up!

Three Friends in the Hot Seat

(Daniel 3)

People are afraid of a lot of things: snakes, heights, storms. But the most common fear, or phobia, is being afraid of what other people think of you. You might have felt this kind of fear before at a piano recital or if you needed to talk in front of group of people. Worrying that people may think you're weird or not good enough can make you want to curl up in a corner.

We can sometimes feel scared to share our faith in God when we are around people who don't believe in Him. But you know what? You don't need to be afraid!

DID YOU KNOW?

You never need to be afraid to stand with God!

Shadrach, Meshach, and Abednego were three friends who loved God and were living in a country where most people did not share their beliefs. When they refused to worship King Nebuchadnezzar instead of God, they had to worry not only about what other people would think of them but what people would do to them.

Because they stood up for their beliefs, Shadrach, Meshach, and Abednego were thrown into a fiery furnace. But in that moment, God stood up for them and saved them from the flames! Even Nebuchadnezzar couldn't deny the power of God.

WORDS TO KNOW!

For I am not ashamed of this Good News about Christ. It is the power of God at work, saving everyone who believes–the Jew first and also the Gentile. Romans 1:16 NLT

And just like Shadrach, Meshach, and Abednego stood up for what they believed in, you don't need to be afraid to stand up for what you believe in too. God will always stand with you!

TALK ABOUT IT!

What are some things you are afraid of? Why are you afraid of them?

Dear God,

Thank You that You are always with us. Help us never to be ashamed of believing in You. Amen.

DO IT!

You never need to be afraid to stand with God!

Daniel and the Friendly Lions

(Daniel 6)

Have you ever tried to teach a dog to obey a command like "sit" or "stay" or "lie down"? It takes a lot of patience and a lot of treats. But eventually, with time, you can train your dog to listen to your commands. Some very brave and skilled people can also do this with lions. But because lions are wild animals, and because they are much bigger and much more dangerous than family dogs, it takes a very long time to train them, and the lion can never be fully trusted not to eat you.

But with God, it's a different story. He made lions, and they will listen and obey Him and His angels right away!

DID YOU KNOW?
God is the King of Kings!

Daniel was a friend of Shadrach, Meshach, and Abednego, and like his three friends, he stood up for what he believed in. When others told him he was not allowed to pray to God, he did it anyway, knowing that obeying God is more important than following man's laws.

For this, Daniel was thrown into the lions' den. Daniel was not a lion tamer and the lions were very hungry, but God sent an angel to keep Daniel safe all night. When Daniel was pulled out of the den the next day, he didn't have even one scratch!

WORDS TO KNOW!
"O Sovereign LORD! You made the heavens and earth by your strong hand and powerful arm. Nothing is too hard for you!" Jeremiah 32:17 NLT

God made everything: the heavens, the earth, people, animals, angels. He is king over everything. And nothing is too hard for Him!

TALK ABOUT IT!

Is there a time when God has protected you and kept you safe?

Dear God,

Nothing is too hard for You. Thank You for loving us and taking care of us. Thank You also for making lions. They are super cool. Amen.

Jonah and the Great Fish

(Jonah 1-4)

Has someone ever treated you unfairly or unkindly? Maybe your big sister didn't invite you to play with her? Maybe a kid at school made fun of you? Do you remember how you felt and what you wanted to do? Some people might want to run away and cry. Others might not say anything and just be mad. And others might want to be mean right back.

When we do something that goes against God's instructions for our lives, it's called sin. Sin hurts our relationship with God, just like our relationships are hurt when we are mean to each other. But when we sin, God does not run away and cry, or sit and stew, or sin right back at us. He has mercy on us and forgives us.

DID YOU KNOW?

God always shows us mercy when we turn to Him!

Jonah knew that God is full of compassion and mercy. Unfortunately, Jonah was not. Jonah knew that if the people of Nineveh, who were enemies of the people of Israel, confessed their sins and turned to God, He would have mercy on them and forgive them. Jonah, however, wanted to see them destroyed, so he ran the other way!

But even though Jonah sinned by going against God's instructions, God had mercy on him. God sent a big fish to swallow up Jonah and then spit him back up on dry ground so that he could finish his job.

In the end, Jonah was right. The people of Nineveh confessed their sin and turned to God, and He had mercy on them!

WORDS TO KNOW!

If we confess our sins, he is faithful and just and will forgive us our sinsand purify us from all unrighteousness.
1 John 1:9 NIV

God will always show us mercy when we turn to Him. And we should also show mercy to each other.

TALK ABOUT IT!

What would it be like to be stuck in a fish for three days? What would you do?

DO IT!

Practice mercy with your family and friends. If they are unfair or unkind to you, don't let that stop you from being fair and kind to them.

Dear God,

Thank You for Your compassion and mercy. Please help us to show mercy to others. Amen.

26 Gabriel Visits Mary and Joseph

(Luke 1:26-38; Matthew 1:18-25)

When the angel Gabriel visited Mary and Joseph, he had some pretty unbelievable news to share. First he told Mary that God had chosen her to bring a baby, His very own Son, into the world. Then he told Joseph, "Don't be afraid to marry Mary. She's pregnant with God's Son."

DID YOU KNOW?
God chose Mary and Joseph to help with His plan!

How did Mary and Joseph react to Gabriel's news? Well, naturally, they were scared at first. But even though they didn't completely understand, they each chose to serve the Lord. And as a result, we are still talking about them today, as part of God's greatest plan to save the world.

When God calls us into His plans and purposes, it's normal to be a little scared. And it's totally fine to have questions—God can answer every single one. But in the end, being a part of the plan and purpose that God calls us to is the very best place to be!

TALK ABOUT IT!

What would have happened to Mary and Joseph if they had said no to Gabriel and to God?

Dear God,

Thank You for Your plan to save us by sending Your Son, Jesus. Please help us to say yes to Your plans, no matter how unbelievable they may be. Amen.

DO IT!

Think about one thing that God has called us to do. It could be loving your neighbor, worshiping Him, or getting to know His Word—or anything else you can think of. Spend some time, today, doing that one thing and saying yes to what God has called you to do!

God with Us

(Matthew 1:25; Luke 2:1-20)

When Jesus was born on that night in Bethlehem, God had come to be with us on earth in human form. Jesus was to be called "Immanuel," meaning "God is with us."

God had sent His own Son to earth, to walk with us, to be an example for us, and to be the ultimate sacrifice for our sins. Soon after that sacrifice, Jesus would go back to

DID YOU KNOW?

God is always with us!

heaven to be with God. Still, He sent His promised Helper, the Holy Spirit (John 15:26), to stay with us on earth, helping us and guiding us as we learn more about God and teach others about Him.

There has never been a time that God has not been with us. John 1:1 tells how He was here in the beginning. And in Revelation, Jesus says, "I am the Alpha and the Omega, the First and the Last, the Beginning and the End" (Revelation 22:13 NCV).

WORDS TO KNOW!

"She will have a son, and they will name him Immanuel," which means "God is with us."
Matthew 1:23 NCV

God was here before the earth was even made. He was here on earth that starry night in Bethlehem. And He will be with us throughout eternity. He is and will always be Immanuel, God with us.

DO IT!

Go outside and look around. Where is God? Can you see Him? How do you know that He is there?

Dear God,

Thank You for caring enough about us to be with us always. Thank You for sending Your Son to be an example for us. Help us to remember that example and that You are always right here with us, from now until eternity. Amen.

Wise Men Worship Jesus

(Matthew 2:1-12)

Around the time Jesus was born, some really smart men who studied the stars and planets saw a brilliantly bright star in the sky. They knew it was the star that led to the Messiah, the Savior who had been written about and talked about for centuries. So they stopped what they were doing, loaded their animals with supplies, and followed the star that led to Jesus.

DID YOU KNOW?

God invites us to worship Him!

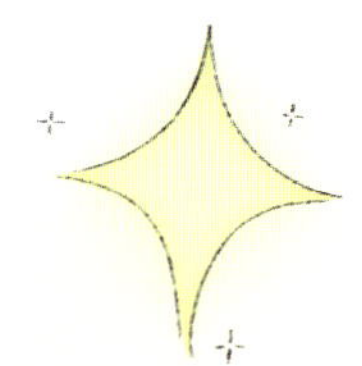

The wise men traveled for a long time, following the star, searching for the Messiah. When they found Him, they bowed low and offered their most precious gifts to Him: gold, frankincense, and myrrh. They worshiped Him.

WORDS TO KNOW!

"Where is the newborn King of the Jews? We saw his star as it rose, and we have come to worship him." Matthew 2:2 NLT

God still invites us to worship Him, and if we are wise, we'll follow His invitation and do just that. We'll stop what we're doing and put Him first. We'll offer our finest gifts, whatever they may be. And we will worship Him.

TALK ABOUT IT!

What are some ways that we worship Jesus?

Dear Jesus,

You are amazing and worthy of worship and praise. Help **us** always to make time to worship You with all that **we** are and all that **we** have. Amen.

DO IT!

Give a gift to Jesus. You may not have any gold, frankincense, or myrrh, but use your gifts and your time to worship Him. Make time to honor Him today and every day.

Jesus in His Father's House

(Luke 2:41-50)

Have you ever gotten separated from your parents at the store or in a crowd? This happened to Jesus when He was twelve years old. His parents were on their way home from the Passover Feast in Jerusalem when they realized Jesus was nowhere to be found in their group walking home. They looked everywhere and asked everyone if they had seen Jesus.

DID YOU KNOW?
Jesus, the Son of God, loved to learn in His Father's house!

After three long days, they finally found Him, listening to the teachers in the temple. Mary, His mother, said what any mother would say: "We've been looking for You everywhere!" Twelve-year-old Jesus simply answered, "Didn't you know I'd be in My Father's house?"

WORDS TO KNOW!

"Why were you searching for me?" he asked. "Didn't you know I had to be in my Father's house?" Luke 2:49 NIV

Jesus' answer is a little funny (unless, of course, you're the mom in this story). But it also makes a powerful point. We get so caught up in the tasks and busyness of life that sometimes we can miss the obvious. We can miss the most important thing. We can miss the opportunity to sit at the feet of our Father, to be in His house, and to learn from Him.

Let's be like Jesus. Let's make it a priority to learn from our Father and to spend time in our Father's house.

TALK ABOUT IT!

What have you learned in the Father's house?

Dear God,

Thank You for giving us wise teachers and leaders in Your house. Help us to thirst for Your knowledge and hunger for Your Word. Help us to make it a priority to be found in Your house. Amen.

DO IT!

You don't have to go to a building to spend time with God. Grab your Bible and go to a quiet place. Set a timer for fifteen minutes, and just sit at your Father's feet, learning, praying, and spending time with Him.

30

Jesus Is Baptized

(Luke 1; Matthew 3; John 1)

John the Baptist was a little weird—in the best way ever! He wore clothes made from camel's hair and ate locusts and honey. But he was also weird in the way he talked about Jesus.

DID YOU KNOW?

John the Baptist was bold in telling people about Jesus!

For hundreds of years, the prophets told of a coming Messiah. People thought He might be a mighty warrior or a wealthy king. And although Jesus was both of those things, it wasn't in the way the world expected. So when Jesus came walking toward John, asking to be baptized along with everyone else, John made sure to tell the crowd exactly who Jesus was: the Lamb of God who would take away the sin of the world.

WORDS TO KNOW!

The next day John saw Jesus coming toward him and said, "Look, the Lamb of God, who takes away the sin of the world!"
John 1:29 NIV

Because of John's bold approach, many believed in Jesus and were baptized in His name. So whenever we feel like we're being weird or a little too loud about Jesus, we can remember John and the difference he made by being bold for Jesus.

TALK ABOUT IT!

Who told you about Jesus? How has it changed your life?

DO IT!

Tell someone about Jesus. You can write a note, sing a song, or share a Bible verse. But find a way to tell someone about Jesus today!

Dear Jesus,

Thank You for the example of John the Baptist. Help us to speak boldly for You, knowing the power of change and forgiveness that You bring to our lives. Thank You for saving us. Amen.

31

Jesus Stands Up to Evil

(Matthew 4:1-11)

After Jesus was baptized, He went to the wilderness and fasted. He didn't eat anything for forty days. His body was weak and hungry.

The devil thought that was the perfect time to tempt Jesus, and that's just what he did. But no matter what Satan said—even when he tempted a very hungry Jesus with bread—Jesus fought back.

DID YOU KNOW?
We can use the power of God's Word just like Jesus did.

Jesus didn't fight Satan with a sword. He didn't throw rocks at him or call him names. Jesus fought back with the Word of God. Because Jesus knew God's Word so well, He had an answer for every tempting thing the devil threw at Him.

WORDS TO KNOW!

Jesus said to him, "Away from me, Satan! For it is written: 'Worship the Lord your God, and serve him only.'" Matthew 4:10 NIV

Satan still roams around today, trying to tempt us with what he thinks we want the most (1 Peter 5:8). But the good news is, we can still fight back the same way that Jesus did: with the powerful, undefeatable Word of God. When we know the absolute truth of what God says in His Word, we won't believe Satan when he comes at us with his lies. We can stand on God's truth, and His truth will set us free (John 8:32).

TALK ABOUT IT!

What are some ways that Satan tempts us? How can we be ready?

Dear Jesus,

Thank You for showing us how to fight Satan's temptation. Help us to study and know Your Word so that we can be ready for whatever the devil throws our way. Thank You for the strength and power of Your Word. Amen.

DO IT!

Make a shield. Get a piece of cardboard or paper and (with help and permission, if needed) cut out the shape of a shield. Now decorate that shield with a powerful scripture (like one of the ones above) you can use to fight back when Satan comes your way.

The Disciples Follow Jesus

(Luke 5:1-11, 27-28; 6:12-16; Matthew 9:9; John 1:35-50)

When Jesus recruited people to teach and help with His ministry, He didn't choose the oldest, wisest people with the best education. He didn't go to church and recruit all the preachers. He called young, smelly fishermen, a tax collector, and even a traitor.

DID YOU KNOW?
The disciples dropped everything to follow Jesus.

Jesus didn't ask to see their report cards or trophies. Jesus didn't give them a quiz on the Ten Commandments. Jesus simply said, "Follow Me." The ones who made excuses missed out. And when He did, they dropped what they were doing and followed Jesus. As a result, they became part of the greatest story ever, learning and witnessing and helping to do the most unbelievable things this side of heaven.

WORDS TO KNOW!

"Come, follow me," Jesus said, "and I will send you out to fish for people." Matthew 4:19 NIV

If you want the adventure of a lifetime, if you want the fullest life there has ever been, if you want to experience a love unlike any this world has to offer, when Jesus calls you, drop everything. Follow Him.

TALK ABOUT IT!

What do you think it means to "fish for people"?

Dear Jesus,

Thank You for calling us to be a part of Your story. **We** want to follow wherever You lead. **We** want to learn how to fish for people. **We** will follow. Amen.

DO IT!

Create a fishing game using a pencil (or stick) for a pole, some string (or dental floss) tied on the end, tape, handmade paper fish, and your imagination. See how many fish you can catch!

33

One Man Thanks Jesus

(Luke 17:11-19)

When ten men asked Jesus to heal them from their skin disease, Jesus didn't hesitate to answer their request. He told them to go show the priests that their disease was gone, and as they were walking, their sores disappeared. Jesus simply spoke, and the men were healed. It was a miracle!

DID YOU KNOW?

Jesus wants us to be thankful!

Ten men received a miraculous gift from Jesus that day. But only *one* man turned around and went back to thank Him.

God has given us so many miraculous gifts. At the top of that list is His very own Son, Jesus, who offers forgiveness for our sins. Let us never make the mistake of being "the other nine." Let us always take the time to notice the gifts we have been given. And let us be the thankful ones.

TALK ABOUT IT!

What are some of the things that God has given you?

Dear Jesus,

You have done so many miracles in our lives. Thank You. Please forgive us when we are ungrateful. And help us to live a life of thankfulness toward You. Amen.

DO IT!

Make a list of things that you are thankful for. Tell God, "Thank You!" for each and every one.

34 The Sermon on the Mount

(Matthew 5-7)

In Jesus' short time on earth, He taught us so much. He not only taught us with His examples of compassion and sacrifice, but He also taught crowds and crowds of people with His words. One of His longest recorded sermons was the Sermon on the Mount.

DID YOU KNOW?

Jesus taught us so much about God's Kingdom!

In that sermon He taught about keeping God's law and giving to the poor and how to pray. He taught about forgiveness. He taught us not to worry. He taught us to treat others as we want to be treated. And that was just one sermon.

WORDS TO KNOW!

"But seek first the kingdom of God and His righteousness, and all these things shall be added to you." Matthew 6:33 NKJV

Jesus shared a wealth of wisdom each time He spoke. Thankfully, His disciples were listening and took the time to write down Jesus' words for us. They have been carefully passed down for centuries so that even now, today, we can learn from the words of Jesus just as the listeners on that mountain did so long ago.

TALK ABOUT IT!

What do you think is the most important wisdom that Jesus shared? Why?

DO IT!

Choose your favorite piece of Jesus' wisdom. Can you think of any examples or songs that help to explain His teaching? Now stand on the nearest mount—or a stool or the front steps of your house—and share your sermon of wisdom.today!

Dear Jesus:

Thank You for sharing all of Your wise words with us. Help us not only to treasure those words in our hearts but also to put those words to work in our lives. Amen.

35

Jesus Feeds Five Thousand

(John 6:1-14)

When a big crowd showed up to hear Jesus speak, the disciples panicked. "There's no way we can feed all these people!" they cried. But Jesus calmly took the five loaves of bread and two fish that a boy had brought. Jesus thanked God for the food and He told the disciples to start passing it out to the people.

WORDS TO KNOW!

Then Jesus took the loaves of bread, thanked God for them, and gave them to the people who were sitting there. John 6:11 NCV

More than five thousand people were fed that day—with five loaves of bread and two fish. Jesus showed that day that God can multiply our offerings to do miraculous things!

So when you're faced with a situation when you don't think you have enough, you have two choices. You can respond like the disciples and panic. Or you can respond like Jesus. You can thank God for what you have—and then step back and watch God do some big things with your little offering.

TALK ABOUT IT!

How have you seen God make a whole lot out of just a little?

Dear Jesus,

Thank You for showing us how to trust God to provide. No matter how small our offerings, thank You for taking them and doing miraculous things. Amen.

DO IT!

At your next meal, look at the food you've been given. Then thank God for always providing you with enough.

36

Above the Waves

(Matthew 14:22-33; Mark 6:45-52; John 6:16-21)

Do you know how to swim? Maybe before you learned how, your mom or dad stood in the pool and asked you to jump in to them. "Don't worry!" your mom or dad said. "I'll catch you!"

It can be scary jumping into the water for the first time, but when you know Mom or Dad is there to catch you, you know you will be okay. And aren't you glad you jumped? Swimming is fun, right?

One night the disciples were in the middle of a lake when

DID YOU KNOW?

You can trust Jesus, who is always there for you!

the wind grew strong. As they fought the waves crashing around them, Jesus, who had been praying on a nearby hill, came toward them. But He didn't come to them in another boat. He walked out to them on top of the water!

Peter was amazed when he saw Jesus coming and asked if he could walk out to meet Him. Peter got out of the boat and walked toward Jesus, but the second he took his eyes off of Jesus, he began to sink! He must have wondered, *How am I walking on the water? This is impossible!*

Right away, Jesus reached out and pulled him up. Peter didn't understand how he could walk on the water, but he did know that he could always trust Jesus.

WORDS TO KNOW!

Trust in the LORD with all your heart; do not depend on your own understanding.
Proverbs 3:5 NLT

We can trust Jesus too! He promises to always be with us. We just need to keep our eyes on Him!

DO IT!

Jump into the pool. If you haven't learned to swim yet, make sure Mom or Dad is there to catch you!

TALK ABOUT IT!

If you were Peter, would you have gotten out of the boat and tried to walk toward Jesus?

Dear God:

Thank You for being with us. Please help us to always keep our eyes on You. Amen.

37 Who Is Your Neighbor?

(Luke 10:25-37)

Have you ever had to go to a new school or make friends in a new neighborhood? Maybe someone has just moved into your neighborhood or school. Meet your new neighbor. It doesn't matter where you came from, what you look, what language you speak, or how different you are from each other, you are each other's neighbors. And you can treat each other with kindness and compassion—just like the good Samaritan!

DID YOU KNOW?

Our neighbor can be anyone, no matter where they come from!

Jesus told a story of a man who was beat up, robbed, and left for dead on the side of the road. People from the man's own town passed by him, and even though they saw that he was injured and in need of help, they did nothing. Then a person from another town walked by.

The people of this man's town were enemies of the people of the injured man's town. But you know what? This man, the good Samaritan, stopped and helped. He treated the injured man with kindness and compassion even though he was different.

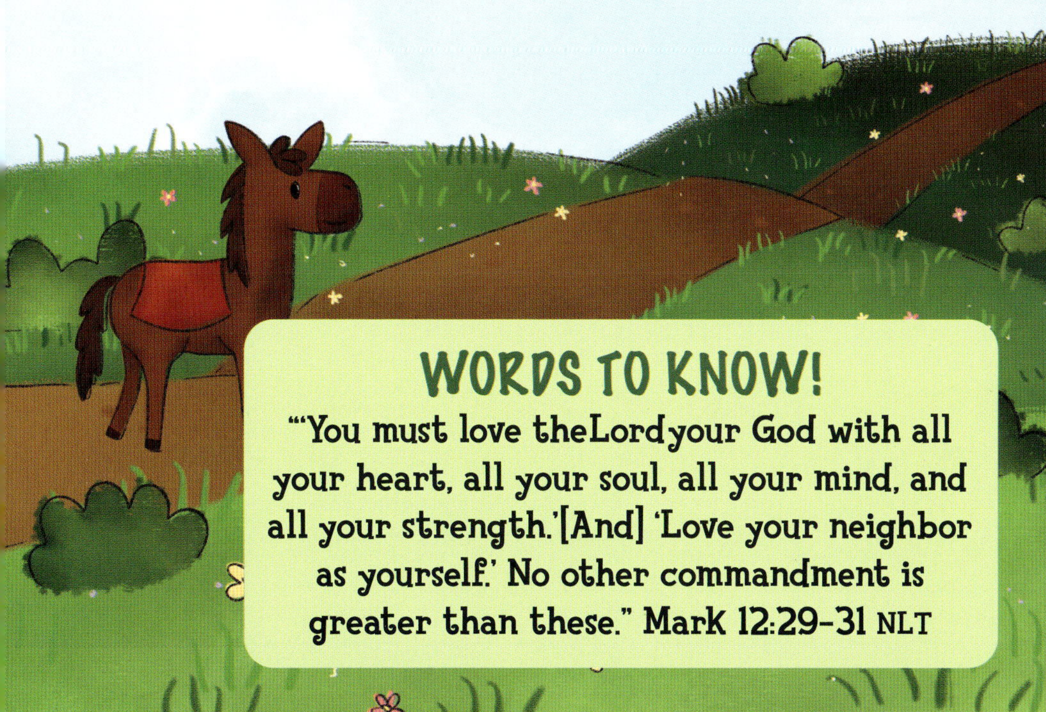

WORDS TO KNOW!

"'You must love the Lord your God with all your heart, all your soul, all your mind, and all your strength.' [And] 'Love your neighbor as yourself.' No other commandment is greater than these." Mark 12:29-31 NLT

This is what it means to love your neighbor. And loving your neighbor is just as important as loving God!

You can be a good neighbor too, no matter your differences!

TALK ABOUT IT!

What would you do if you saw that someone was hurt and needed help?

Dear Jesus,

Please help us
to always be a
good neighbor
to everyone. And
when we need help,
please send a good
neighbor our way.
Amen.

DO IT!

Bring some cookies
to your next-door
neighbor.

38

Sibling Rivalry

(Luke 10:38-42)

You love your mom, right?! Of course you do. She's awesome!

Imagine it's Mother's Day and you've come up with two ideas for a present. You'll let her choose the one she wants. Idea number one is that she'll go out on a bike ride by herself all day while you stay home and clean the house and do all the laundry. Idea number two is that you'll both go on a bike ride, have a picnic, go swimming, and spend the day together.

Which one do you think she'll pick?

DID YOU KNOW?

Spending time with Jesus is more important than doing things for Him!

Of course she'd appreciate you cleaning the house and doing all the laundry, but she'll most likely pick idea two. Why? Because she loves you and wants to spend time with you. Her relationship with you is more important!

When Jesus came to visit the home of two sisters, Mary and Marth, Martha stayed busy cooking and serving the guests in their house while Mary sat at Jesus' feet and listened to Him teach. Martha became upset that she was doing all the work while her sister relaxed. Martha asked Jesus to tell Mary to help her. But Jesus told Martha that Mary was doing exactly what she should be doing: spending time with Him.

Jesus loves us and wants to spend time with us. Our relationship with Him is the most important thing!

WORDS TO KNOW!

"Then you will call on me and come and pray to me, and I will listen to you. You will seek me and find me when you seek me with all your heart." Jeremiah 29:12–13 NIV

The best way to spend time with Jesus is by seeking Him in prayer.

TALK ABOUT IT!

Why is it important to spend time *with* God? Why is it more important than doing things *for* Him?

Dear Jesus,

Thank You that we can find You when we seek You with all our heart. Thank You for listening to **our** prayers. Please help **us** to grow closer to You. Amen.

The Wind and the Waves Obey Him

(Matthew 8:23-27; Mark 4:35-41; Luke 8:22-25)

Have you ever been on a beach with big waves? If you go too far out and one of those waves crashes over you, there's nothing you can do but roll around under the water like a floppy doll. Forget about trying to swim; the water is just too powerful. You'll just have to wait for the wave to recede before you can stand up and get back to land.

The wind can also be super powerful. Hurricanes and tornadoes can lift cars into the air and blow whole houses to the ground. You can't do anything to stop the wind. The only thing you can do is get to a safe place and wait for the storm to pass.

DID YOU KNOW?

God is in control of everything!

But the waves and the wind are not too powerful for God. Fire, hail, snow and clouds, wind and weather obey Him.

The disciples were terrified when they were caught in a boat during a big storm at sea. Jesus was sleeping in the boat, and the disciples wondered why He wasn't worried too. They woke up Jesus, afraid they were all going to drown. Jesus stood and commanded the sea, "Silence! Be still!" (Mark 4:39 nlt). Immediately, the waves flattened and the wind stopped. The disciples were amazed. "'Who is this man?' they asked each other. "Even the winds and the waves obey him!" (Mark 4:41 NLT). You know the answer. The Son of God, that's who!

WORDS TO KNOW!

Praise the LORD from the earth, you creatures of the ocean depths, fire and hail, snow and clouds, wind and weather that obey him. Psalm 148:7-8 NLT

God is bigger and more powerful than anything in creation. He commands it all!

TALK ABOUT IT!

What do you think surprised the disciples more: to see Jesus walking on the water or to see the storm stop when He ordered it to?

Dear Jesus:

The wind and the waves
obey You. We praise You.
All creation praises You.
Your glory towers over
earth and heaven. Amen.

DO IT!

From inside your house, watch a thunderstorm as the rain pours and the lightning flashes.

The Great Physician

(Matthew 9:18-26; Mark 5:21-43; Luke 8:40-56)

Sometimes when we want something really badly, we pray and ask God to give us what we want. Maybe it's a new toy or to go on a trip. Perhaps you want God's help to pass a test or not to get into trouble. What about praying for help for someone you love? Does your dad need to find a new job or is your friend sick? God loves it when we pray because we are talking to Him. He wants to be close to us.

Both the sick woman and Jairus had great faith in Jesus. The woman believed that Jesus could heal her sickness and Jairus knew that Jesus could save his daughter. Jesus told the woman, "The faith you have in Me has healed you." And He told Jairus, "Don't be afraid. Have faith. Your little girl is not dead. She is only sleeping." Jesus answered their prayers and everyone was amazed. The One who can command the wind and the waves is also the great healer!

DID YOU KNOW?

God answers your prayers!

WORDS TO KNOW!

"But if you remain in me and my words remain in you, you may ask for anything you want, and it will be granted!" John 15:7 NLT

The more you pray, the closer you become to God. He wants you talk to Him and to trust that He will answer your prayers!

TALK ABOUT IT!

Do you need to ask God for help with anything in your life? How about for a friend or someone in your family?

Dear Jesus,

We thank You that You have the power to heal. And we thank You that You answer our prayers when we trust in You. Amen.

DO IT!

Pray the Lord's Prayer every day for a whole week. You can find the Lord's Prayer in your Bible in Matthew 6:9-13.

Let Them Come!

(Matthew 19:14; Mark 10:13–15)

It can be hard to be a kid. Your parents tell you what time you have to go to bed, you're forced to eat vegetables, you sometimes need permission to use the bathroom, and when you get there, you can't reach the faucet. Older kids can look down on you, and some grown-ups might not take you seriously.

DID YOU KNOW?

Jesus loves every single person, no matter how tall or how small!

But you know one of the best things you've got going for you? Humility! When you are not prideful or arrogant and you are kind to other people, you have humility, and most kids are great at being humble!

One day the disciples found out what Jesus thought about children when He was speaking to a large crowd. Parents began sending their children to Jesus to be blessed, and the disciples worried that the kids would bother Jesus. They told the parents that Jesus had more important things to do. Boy, were they wrong!

Jesus got very upset because He loves everyone, no matter their size or age. In fact, He told everyone how special children are. Jesus said, "Let the children come to Me. Don't keep them away! For the Kingdom of Heaven belongs to those who are like these children" (Matthew 19:14 NLT). These children had humility. They wanted to come to Jesus and be blessed by Him.

"So anyone who becomes as humble as this little child is the greatest in the Kingdom of Heaven." Matthew 18:4 NLT

TALK ABOUT IT!

Do you like being around other people who are humble? Why?

Whether you are big or small, a kid or an adult, stay humble and run to Jesus. He loves you very much!

DO IT!

Help your parents with a chore around the house without being asked.

Dear Jesus,

Please help us to stay humble and to remember that we need You. Thank You for loving us when we are small and when we get bigger. Amen.

The Widow's Offering

(Mark 12:38-44; Luke 21:1-4)

A lot of grown-ups worry about money. Maybe you've heard your parents talking about how to pay for repairing a car or how your family isn't going to eat dinner out because it's too expensive. Some grown-ups have a lot of money and can buy new cars or go out to eat whenever they want. But no matter if you have money or not, whether you are rich or you are poor, or somewhere in between, you can trust God for everything!

DID YOU KNOW?
God wants us to trust Him with everything!

Jesus was teaching in the temple in Jerusalem when He saw a rich man throw a bunch of money into the offering box. The rich man was very proud and wanted everyone to see how much money he was giving to God. He felt that because he had plenty, God needed him more than he needed God.

But right behind him was a poor woman who tossed in two coins that were worth less than a penny. The woman had lost everything when her husband died, and this was all that she had. Jesus told His disciples that her penny was worth more than the rich man's whole bag of money! Why? Because the woman realized she needed God and was putting her trust in Him. She knew that God would provide for her needs. She was giving out of a grateful heart, not a proud heart.

WORDS TO KNOW!

Teach those who are rich in this world not to be proud and not to trust in their money, which is so unreliable. Their trust should be in God, who richly gives us all we need for our enjoyment.1 Timothy 6:17 NLT

We can also trust God to take care of us so we can give with a grateful heart!

TALK ABOUT IT!

What are some of the ways God has been generous with you? How has He taken care of you?

Dear God,

Thank You for providing for us. And thank You that we can trust You with everything! Amen.

DO IT!

Donate some of your old toys and clothes to Goodwill or another charity near you.

43

The Lamb of God

(Matthew 26:17-29; Mark 14:12-25; Luke 22:7-20; John 13:1-20)

Do you go to a church that serves communion? Some churches celebrate communion once a month; others do it every week. The pastor or priest will bless the bread and wine (or grape juice) and then the people in the church will eat and drink it. Have you ever wondered why?

Jesus started this tradition at the Last Supper before His death. He wanted His disciples to remember the sacrifice He was making for them. If we love and follow Jesus, when we take communion, we remember what Jesus did for us and thank Him.

DID YOU KNOW?
Jesus is the Lamb of God and He takes away the sins of the world!

When God brought the Israelites out of slavery in Egypt, Moses told the people to sacrifice a lamb and brush its blood around the doors to their houses. The Lord passed through the land to strike down the Egyptians, but He passed over any house where He saw the blood. Anyone who had the blood of the lamb was saved.

John the Baptist called Jesus the Lamb of God, because He would be sacrificed and die so that that we could live. Jesus gave us His body and His blood so that we could live with God forever. Every time we eat the bread and drink the juice at communion, we remember what Jesus did for us.

WORDS TO KNOW!

The next day John [the Baptist] saw Jesus coming toward him and said, "Look! The Lamb of God who takes away the sin of the world!" John 1:29 NLT

If you have asked Jesus into your heart, you can celebrate His gift to us by taking communion.

DO IT!

Ask your parents about celebrating communion at your church.

Dear Jesus,

Thank You for loving us so much that You would die for us! Thank You for Your sacrifice, and help **us** always to remember what You did for **us**. Amen.

TALK ABOUT IT!

How does your church celebrate communion? Talk to your pastor or priest about why it's celebrated that way.

44 A Lonely Night in the Garden

(Matthew 26:30, 36–56; Mark 14:26, 32–52; Luke 22:39–53; John 18:1–12)

Have you ever been sad? The answer is yes. Everybody has been sad at one time or another. Maybe you were a little sad when you didn't get the toy you wanted, or when you wanted to stay up and play but your parents made you go to bed. Sometimes that kind of sadness doesn't last long. But if you've had a pet or a friend or a family member die, that can make you really sad for a long time. One of the best things to do when you are feeling sad—whether it's a little or a lot—is to pray to your heavenly Father. That's what Jesus did.

DID YOU KNOW?

When Jesus was hurting, He spent time in prayer talking with His Father.

Right after the Last Supper, Jesus went to a garden with His disciples to pray. He was very sad because He knew that soon He would die. Jesus asked Peter, James, and John to stay with Him and keep watch while He prayed. Even though Jesus did not want to suffer, He prayed that whatever His Father wanted Him to do, He would do.

An angel then came to help strengthen Jesus. And though Jesus was overwhelmed with sorrow, He kept praying to His Father. Jesus prayed so long and so late that Peter, James, and John could not stay awake. Jesus woke up His friends two different times to remind them that they also needed to stay up and pray; they were going to need God's help too.

When Jesus had finished praying early in the morning, the Roman soldiers came to arrest Him.

WORDS TO KNOW!

The LORD is close to the brokenhearted; he rescues those whose spirits are crushed. Psalm 34:18 NLT

If your heart is broken, go to your heavenly Father in prayer. He rescues those whose spirits are crushed.

TALK ABOUT IT!

Why do you think God wants us to pray?

Dear God,

Thank You that
we can talk to You
whether we are happy
or sad. Thank You for
strengthening and
comforting us. And
like Jesus, help us to
do what You want.
Amen.

DO IT!

Find a quiet spot outside and say a prayer.

Jesus Dies

(Matthew 27; Mark 15; Luke 22:66-71; John 18:28-19:42)

Every year, two days before Easter Sunday, we celebrate Good Friday. When you hear the story of what happened on Good Friday, you might wonder why it's not called "Very Bad Friday." If you have ever visited a large church or cathedral, you might have noticed stained glass pictures or carvings that tell the story about what happened that Friday. When you look at the images, you feel more sad than happy, but what happened on this day was necessary for the celebration to come.

DID YOU KNOW?
The reason Jesus came to earth was to give His life for us.

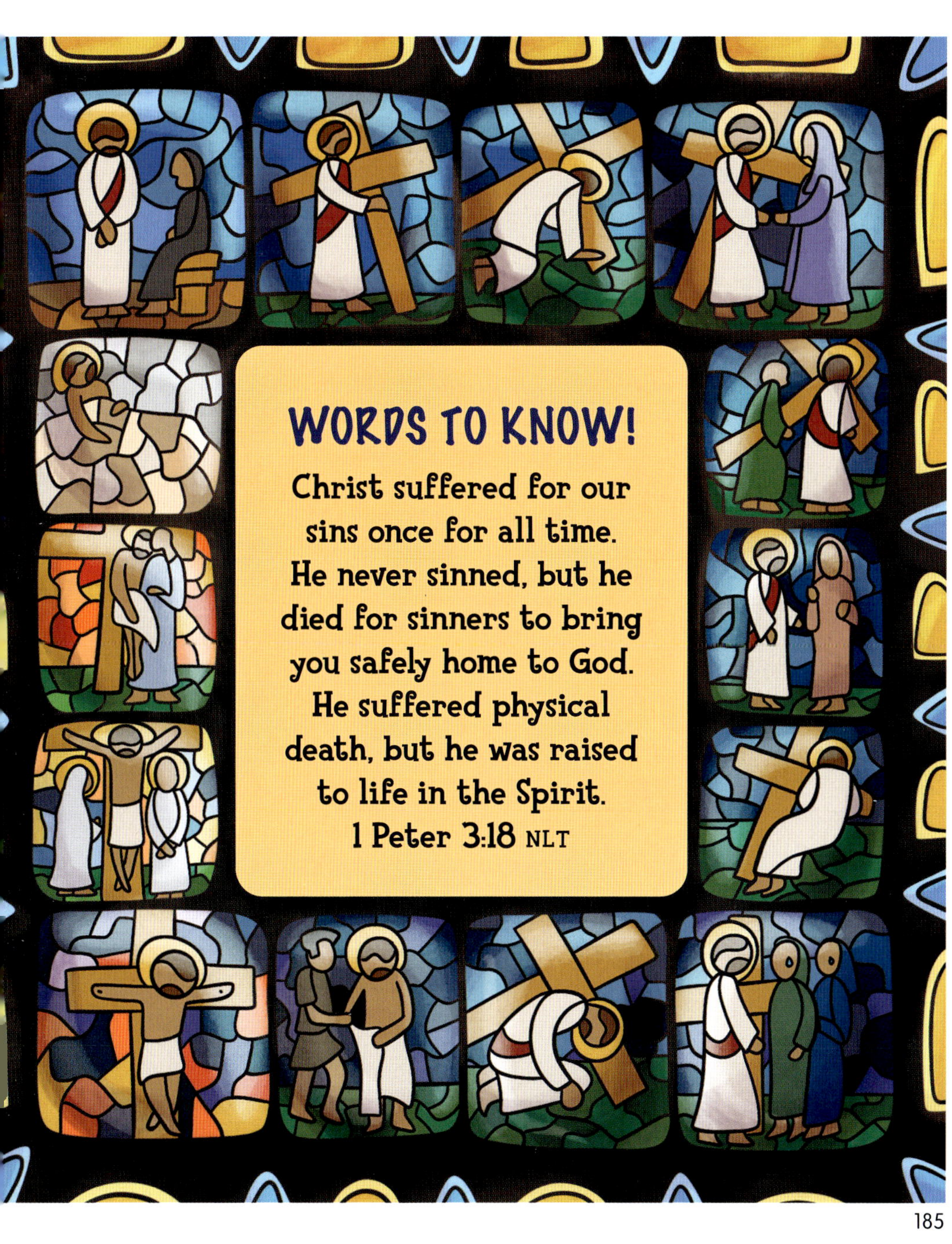

WORDS TO KNOW!

Christ suffered for our
sins once for all time.
He never sinned, but he
died for sinners to bring
you safely home to God.
He suffered physical
death, but he was raised
to life in the Spirit.
1 Peter 3:18 NLT

It's called Good Friday, even though many bad things happened, because the reason Jesus came to earth was to suffer and die for our sins so that we could live with God forever. And that is very good!

TALK ABOUT IT!

Why do you think it's important to remember and think about what happened on Good Friday?

Dear God,

Thank You for sending Your Son to die so that we can live. Help **us** always to remember what You did for **us** on that Good Friday. Amen.

DO IT!

Find and visit a church in your community with the stations of the cross. And you don't have to do it on Good Friday!

Jesus Is Alive!

(Matthew 28:1–15; Mark 16:1–12; Luke 24; John 20)

What is your favorite thing about Easter? Is it the egg hunt when you search for plastic eggs filled with candy? Maybe it's coloring and decorating actual eggs with your mom or waking up to find a basket filled with all kinds of goodies on Easter morning. Or it might be going to church in your best clothes and then having a big lunch with your family and friends.

DID YOU KNOW?

Jesus defeated the power of death!

There are so many fun things about Easter because it is truly a day to celebrate! Christmas, the day Jesus came to earth, and Easter, the day when Jesus rose from the dead, are the two most joyful holidays of the whole year!

Jesus was born, lived a life without sin, then paid the price for our sin when He died for us. But that's not all. The grave could not hold Him! Jesus defeated the power of sin and death once and for all when He came back to earth three days after He died. God did this because of His great love or us. "For this is how God loved the world: He gave his one and only Son, so that everyone who believes in him will not perish but have eternal life" (John 3:16 NLT).

WORDS TO KNOW!

Then the angel spoke to the women. "Don't be afraid!" he said. "I know you are looking for Jesus, who was crucified.He isn't here! He is risen from the dead, just as He said would happen." Matthew 28:5-6 NLT

This is the best news of all and the very best reason to celebrate!

Dear God,

Thank You that You loved us so much that You sent us Your Son. Thank You that Jesus defeated sin and death and that **we** can live with You forever! Amen.

DO IT!

Color eggs with your family to remind you of Easter. It doesn't matter what time of the year it is!

The Good News

(Matthew 28:16-20)

The disciples had just witnessed the most amazing thing ever. After years of miraculous ministry, Jesus, their teacher and friend, had died on a cross. And three days later, He rose to life again! Then for forty days after Jesus came back, the disciples sat at the feet of their teacher, soaking in every word.

DID YOU KNOW?
Jesus asked us to share the best news in the world!

Before Jesus went back to heaven, He gave the disciples their "Great Commission," the job He wanted them to do while He was in heaven. "Go tell the whole world about Me! Tell them what you have seen! Baptize them in My name!"

WORDS TO KNOW!

"Therefore, go and make disciples of all the nations, baptizing them in the name of the Father and the Son and the Holy Spirit." Matthew 28:19 NLT

Did you know that Jesus calls us to do the same? We've seen His miracles, heard His wisdom, and know the forgiveness He brings. And until the whole world knows about Jesus, it is our job to carry on the work of His disciples: to spread the word of the best news ever!

TALK ABOUT IT!

What are some ways that you can share the good news about Jesus?

Dear Jesus,

Thank You for offering us forgiveness and eternal life in heaven. It's the best news ever! Help us never to stop sharing that news until the whole world hears! Amen.

DO IT!

Who do you know who hasn't heard the good news about Jesus? Make a list or draw a picture of them, and let it remind you to pray for them every day. Ask God to show you the best way to share the good news with them.

Jesus Goes to Heaven

(Luke 24; Acts 1)

The disciples had seen Jesus do countless miracles. They had seen Him die on a cross. And they had seen Him risen to life again. They had learned so much from Him. They had grown to trust Him and love Him. But now it was time to say goodbye.

DID YOU KNOW?
The disciples didn't just wait on Jesus—they went out and got to work!

After Jesus descended into heaven, the disciples stood there looking at the sky, waiting. Then two men in bright white clothes appeared and said, "Why are you still standing there?" That's when the disciples remembered the job that Jesus had given them, and they went straight to work.

WORDS TO KNOW!

"Why do you stand here looking into the sky? This same Jesus, who has been taken from you into heaven, will come back in the same way you have seen him go into heaven." Acts 1:11 NIV

We should do the same. Sure, the more time we spend with Him, the stronger we will be in doing our work in the world for Him. But we can't just stand around waiting for Jesus to come back. We need to be hard at work, doing the job He left for us to do!

TALK ABOUT IT!

What are some things we could be doing until Jesus comes back?

DO IT!

Using dolls or toys or building blocks, recreate the scene that day, when the disciples watched Jesus go back home into heaven.

Dear Jesus,

Thank You for Your words and wisdom. And thank You for the work You've given us to do. Help us to have the strength to keep working until You return for us. Amen.

The Disciples Spread the Word

(Acts 2–3, 9, 12, 16)

After Jesus went back to heaven, the disciples received the Helper Jesus had promised (John 14:15–18). With this Helper, they were able to speak other languages and talk to lots of different people about Jesus. When the disciples spoke boldly about Jesus, many believed and were baptized.

DID YOU KNOW?

The disciples spoke boldly about Jesus, and many believed!

The Helper, also called the Holy Spirit, is still here to help us like Jesus did with His disciples. The Holy Spirit helps us to know right from wrong, helps us to pray, and helps us when we're telling others about Jesus. In this way, Jesus is right here with us, helping us to continue to do the work of the disciples.

WORDS TO KNOW!

Peter replied, "Repent and be baptized, every one of you, in the name of Jesus Christ for the forgiveness of your sins." Acts 2:38 NIV

Jesus knew that we would all need a Helper. Things were tough when Jesus was on the earth, and He knew that things would be tough for Christians long after He went back to heaven. But as Christians, we are to speak boldly about Jesus so that others can know Him too. And as Christians, we have everything we need to do that because we believe in the One who has already overcome the world (John 16:33).

TALK ABOUT IT!

How can the Helper make it easier to tell others about Jesus?

Dear Jesus,

Thank You for providing a Helper for us. Help **us** to be like the disciples, boldly telling others about You so that others can know You too. Amen.

DO IT!

Look through John 14, 15, and 16 to see what Jesus tells us about the Helper or the Holy Spirit. Make a list of the ways that Jesus said the Holy Spirit would help us.

John Sees Heaven

(Revelation 1, 4, 21)

What do you imagine when you think of heaven? Jesus told His disciples that He was going to prepare a place for them (John 14:2). The book of Revelation describes in great detail what John saw when Jesus took him to see the new heavens and new earth (Revelation 21:1).

DID YOU KNOW?

God has prepared a place for us to live with Him forever!

John wrote of rainbows and angels. He saw jewels and crowns. He told of a city shining as clear as crystal. Yet, even with all of John's details, it's difficult to imagine exactly what heaven looks like, but we can try.

WORDS TO KNOW!

The One who was sitting on the throne said, "Look! I am making everything new!"
Revelation 21:5 NCV

Even though the details help us to imagine what it would *look* like, the most important, amazing thing is what it will *feel* like. God's warmth and His glory will be so bright that there will be no need for a sun or a moon (Revelation 21:23). And there will be no guilt or sin, nothing to separate us from that glory. Heaven will be joyful and perfect and sinless, and we will be wrapped in the warmth of the glory of God. Forever.

Just imagine.

TALK ABOUT IT!

How do you get to spend eternity in heaven?

Dear Jesus,

Thank You for going to prepare a place where we can live with You forever. Help us to believe in You—and help others to believe in You—so that we can all spend eternity in heaven with You. Amen.

DO IT!

Using John's descriptions in Revelation, draw your favorite scene from heaven. Then take some time to talk to Jesus about spending eternity with Him.